Together
at Mass

First printing, March, 1987
Second printing, March, 1991
60,000 copies in print

Nihil Obstat:
      James T. O'Connor, S.T.D
      Censor Librorum

Imprimatur:
      +Joseph T. O'Keefe, D.D.
      Vicar-General, Archdiocese of New York

The nihil obstat and imprimatur are official declarations that a book or pamphlet is free of doctrinal or moral error. No implication is contained therein that those who have granted the nihil obstat and imprimatur agree with the contents, opinions or statements expressed.

Excerpts from the English translation of *The Roman Missal* © 1973, International Committee on English in the Liturgy, Inc. All rights reserved.

Library of Congress Catalog Card Number: 87-70417

International Standard Book Number: 0-87793-357-X

Text design by Katherine A. Coleman

Printed and bound in the United States of America.

Together at Mass

Gaynell Bordes Cronin
and
Joan Bellina

Illustrations by Betty Murtagh

AVE MARIA PRESS NOTRE DAME, INDIANA 46556

Parents:

The note to parents in the back will help you present *Together at Mass* most effectively to your child.

This book belongs

to: _____

We Celebrate

We come together to celebrate as family around our home table. At Mass we come together to celebrate and worship as God's family. Jesus is present among us.

Introductory Rite

The entrance procession begins this rite and usually consists of ministers with lighted candles, a cross, a reader who may carry the gospel book, and the celebrant. We stand and sing an entrance song to show our oneness as the gathered worshipping community. After the song we make the sign of the cross which reminds us that we have been baptized in the name of the Father, and of the Son and of the Holy Spirit. The celebrant then welcomes us in the name of the Lord with a simple statement that God is present with us. As a united faith community we respond, "And also with you."

In the name of the Father,
and of the Son,
and of the Holy Spirit.
Amen.
The Lord be with you.
And also with you.

We Forgive

Sometimes we hurt others. We say, "I am sorry." At Mass we stop and think about the times we have failed to love. We ask for forgiveness.

The Penitential Rite _____

Before hearing God's word and offering our gifts at the altar, we confess to God and to one another that we are sorry for our failures to grow in love. As people who know we are loved by God, we proclaim our need for forgiveness and for reconciliation by either saying the *Confiteor* or responding "Lord, have mercy" to the invocations spoken by the priest.

We answer the priest by saying:

Lord, have mercy.
Christ, have mercy.
Lord, have mercy.

The Liturgy of the Word

We Listen

At home we learn to listen to one
another. At Mass we listen to readings
from the Bible. God speaks to us
in these words. Jesus comes to us
with the Good News.

The Readings _____

The readings from scripture form the main part of the Liturgy of the Word.
Scripture tells us about the history of salvation and God's love for us. The first
reading is from the Old Testament; the second is from the New Testament.
The third reading, the gospel, tells us about Jesus, what he said and did,
and how the people responded to him. The homily helps us reflect on the
readings and discover how to live God's word in our daily lives.

At the end of the readings, the Reader says:

This is the word of the Lord.

Thanks be to God.

We stand and praise Jesus by singing:

Alleluia!

The Lord be with you.

And also with you.

A reading from the holy gospel according to (Matthew, Mark, Luke or John)

Glory to you, Lord.

After the gospel, the priest says:

This is the gospel of the Lord.

Praise to you,
Lord Jesus Christ.

We Care

At home we care for one another. At
Mass we pray together for the
needs of all the members of God's
family. We ask God's help for all people.

General Intercessions _____

As brothers and sisters we come together and pray in faith for the needs of
all members of the family of God, living and dead. We ask God for help not
only for those present, but for all people—for the church, for civil authorities,
for those oppressed in any way, for all humanity, and for the salvation of the
world. We may pray in our hearts for special individual or family intentions.

After each request we answer,
Lord, hear our prayer.*

*other phrases may be used

The Liturgy of the Eucharist

We Give

We prepare our family table for our meals. Everything we have is a gift from God. At Mass we bring bread and wine to the altar and offer them and ourselves as gifts to God.

Preparation of the Altar and Gifts _____

For this special meal of the Eucharist, we prepare the altar table by placing bread and wine on it. These gifts are brought to the altar by members of the family of God. They show our gratitude for the goods of the earth which we have and use. The money collected for the church and the poor is presented. We should also offer ourselves, bringing all the actions of our daily lives to the altar. The priest receives the gifts and in song or in silence we prepare our hearts for Jesus as we set the parish table of the Lord.

Pray, my brothers and sisters, that our
sacrifice may be acceptable to God, the
almighty Father.

**May the Lord accept the sacrifice at your hands
for the praise and glory of his name,
for our good, and the good of all his Church.**

We Share

We share with others at home. When someone shares with us we say, "Thank you."

At Mass we offer a sacrifice to God by sharing in the sacrifice Jesus offered on the cross.

Now the gifts of bread and wine are ready. The priest prays over them, asking God that they become our food, Jesus. We give thanks for God's love.

The Eucharistic Prayer _____

The word *eucharist* itself literally means "thanksgiving." The element of thanksgiving is clearly focused in the Preface and in the dialogue which leads to the Preface. With hands extended the celebrant invites us to give thanks for all the gifts that God has shared with us. This is the time for us to be thankful for the beauty of creation, the love of people, the presence of Jesus in our lives through the gift of the Spirit. Our response is also a thanksgiving prayer.

The Lord be with you.
And also with you.

Lift up your hearts.
We lift them up to the Lord.
Let us give thanks to the Lord our God.
It is right to give him thanks and praise.
Together people and celebrant sing or say:
Holy, Holy, Holy Lord
God of power and might . . .

We Remember

Jesus loves us. We remember his love as the bread and wine become the body and blood of Jesus.

The Consecration and Memorial Acclamation _____

In the eucharistic meal we remember and give thanks for what Jesus has done; the people gathered meet him now present in the eucharistic elements; and we look forward to the future when we will have the meal of the kingdom. In response to the words of institution we are asked to proclaim the mystery of faith—the mystery of Christ's death, rising and presence among his people. We proclaim our faith through one of the four forms of the Memorial Acclamation.

This is my body. . . .
This is my blood. . . .
We remember that Jesus lived, died and
rose, and with the priest we say:

Christ has died.
Christ is risen.
Christ will come again.*

We say yes to Jesus in our life as we sing or say:

Amen.

*Sometimes we say another form of this prayer.

We Belong

We belong together. We are family.
We show our oneness with Jesus
and with all our brothers and sisters.
We pray the Our Father, and we offer
a sign of peace to one another.

The Lord's Prayer and the Sign of Peace _____

We are brothers and sisters in God's family; we are responsible for one another. Our mission, like Jesus', is to make all people one. The Our Father is the special prayer of God's family, taught to us by Jesus himself.

At the Sign of Peace we offer both words and gestures to one another—a handshake, a nod, a hug or a kiss. Through these words and actions we express our love and friendship for all the people present, and we remember our call to become peacemakers in our world.

Our Father who art in heaven
hallowed be thy name.
Thy kingdom come.
Thy will be done on earth as it is in heaven.
Give us this day our daily bread,
and forgive us our trespasses
as we forgive those who trespass against us.
And lead us not into temptation,
but deliver us from evil.

For the kingdom, the power, and the
glory are yours, now and for ever.

The peace of the Lord be with you always.
And also with you.
We turn to those near us and say:
Peace be with you.

We Ask

Everyday we ask questions.
Sometimes we ask others to forgive us.
Sometimes we ask for things that
we want. Jesus is the Lamb of God.
We ask him to forgive us for the
things we do that are wrong. We ask
him to give us peace.

The Breaking of the Bread _____

At the Last Supper Jesus broke bread and shared it with his apostles. On
Good Friday his body was broken for all of us. In the Eucharist we share
Christ's body, broken that we might become one. We ask for mercy and for
peace, now and always.

With the priest we say or sing:

> **Lamb of God, you take away the sins of the world, have mercy on us.**
>
> **Lamb of God, you take away the sins of the world, have mercy on us.**
>
> **Lamb of God, you take away the sins of the world, grant us peace.**

We Receive

When we eat a family meal, we know that everything we have comes from others. At Mass we are now invited to receive our special food, Jesus, in communion.

Communion

The Eucharist is a sacrament of unity. The many grains of wheat that form the one bread speak clearly of how many may be one. As the church, we are the one body of Christ. It is as the body of Christ that we are invited to receive the Eucharist. When we respond "Amen" as the minister offers us the bread of life, we profess our belief in the real presence of Christ in the sacrament of the Eucharist. Through the Eucharist he becomes present in all who receive him and unites them with one another. We receive the body of Christ, and we are the body of Christ.

The body of Christ.
Amen.
The blood of Christ.
Amen.

We Serve

We have come together as God's family. Our love now leads us to go out and serve God by loving and serving one another.

The Closing Blessing _____

The effect of the Eucharist is love, love which leads to the service of others in the name of Jesus. The celebration of the Eucharist does not end with the last words of the liturgy; it continues as we go forth to continue loving, celebrating and serving God in others.

Go in peace to love
and serve the Lord.
Thanks be to God.

Dear Parents,

As you help your child become familiar with the Mass, we hope you will notice that the actions we use in presenting the parts of the Mass—celebrating, forgiving, listening, caring, giving, sharing, remembering, belonging, asking, receiving, serving—are familiar actions of daily life in the family. Your child experiences these actions and can understand the Mass through them.

The explanations which are offered with each part of the Mass are to aid you in reviewing the liturgy as you help your child. We chose to spotlight those parts of the Mass which a young child can most easily recognize and take part in rather than present all the prayers of the Mass. Over the years your child will come to know and appreciate the richness and unity of the eucharistic celebration more completely. For now, we will keep the explanations simple and focus on the prayers which are within the child's attention span and comprehension.

Be sure to look carefully at the pictures with your child. Point out the gestures and expressions of the celebrant and of the people gathered. Ask your child what is going on in these pictures. The Mass is long and "word-oriented" from a child's point of view. Noticing actions, gestures and expressions can be meaningful and interesting, and brings the child into the Mass in a way he or she can readily understand.

Gaynell Bordes Cronin
Joan Bellina